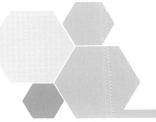

Contents

Contents

Workbook introduction

1 ILM Super Series study links

This workbook addresses the issues of *Leading Your Team*. Should you wish to extend your study to other Super Series workbooks covering related or different subject areas, you will find a comprehensive list at the back of this book.

2 Links to ILM qualifications

This workbook relates to the following learning outcomes in segments from the ILM Level 3 Introductory Certificate in First Line Management and the Level 3 Certificate in First Line Management.

C8.3   Leadership
1   Recognize the difference between leadership and management
2   Identify alternative leadership styles and qualities
3   Know when and how to apply a particular leadership style in the workplace
4   Assess the effects of differing leadership styles on group activities
5   Recognize own preferred leadership style
6   Develop trust within the team.

3 Links to S/NVQs in management

This workbook relates to the following elements of the Management Standards which are used in S/NVQs in Management, as well as a range of other S/NVQs.

C1.1   Develop your own skills to improve your performance
C12.1   Plan the work of teams and individuals
C12.2   Assess the work of teams and individuals
C12.3   Provide feedback to teams and individuals on their work.

It will also help you to develop the following personal competences:

- building teams;
- focusing on results;
- managing self.

4 Workbook objectives

A leader is best
When people barely know that he exists.
Not so good when people obey and acclaim him,
Worst when they despise him.
'Fail to honour people,
They fail to honour you';
But of a good leader, who talks little,
When his work is done, his aim fulfilled,
They will all say, 'We did this ourselves'.
                    Lao-Tzu, Chinese Philosopher, 6th Century BC.[1]

Team leaders are special people. In work organizations, they have the key task of making things happen, not directly, but through the teams they lead. This is a difficult job: one that requires patience, determination, and an ability to motivate.

[1] Quoted in *Effective Leadership* (Extension 1).

Many writers and teachers down the centuries have attempted to define the qualities of leadership. Is it something inherent – something you're born with, or can anyone be a leader? And what does a leader have to do? What techniques can be employed, what actions taken, to turn a collection of individuals into a well-ordered, fully functioning unit?

In this workbook we will try to answer these questions. We'll examine ways in which you, as a team leader, can improve your leadership skills, and so help your team to become more effective.

In Session A, we focus on the attributes of leadership itself, and try to decide which of them can be acquired or learned. An interesting aspect of this is a comparison between the skills needed for management and those which a leader should have. Most managers are expected to be leaders, but is a leader necessarily a manager?

Session B is concerned with just two facets of leadership: responsibilities and roles. We will put forward the view that a leader has three kinds of responsibilities: those to the task, to the team and to the individual team member. This three-fold burden, and the leader's many other duties, may result in role conflict or role ambiguity; we look at this subject at the end of the session.

For Session C, the style of leadership comes under the spotlight. Each individual brings their own skills, attributes, attitudes, strengths and flaws to the team. The leader must be adaptable and adopt a *style* of leadership that is appropriate to the team at that time.

4.1 Objectives

When you have completed this workbook you will be better able to:

- assess your own leadership qualities and potential;
- enhance your leadership skills;
- recognize the responsibilities of leadership, and the roles to be played by a team leader;
- identify and adopt a style of leadership appropriate to the needs of the team and its particular situation.

5 Activity planner

The following activities require some planning so you may want to look at these now.

■ Activity 11   Asks you to demonstrate how effectively you assess the performance of your workteam

■ Activity 31   Asks you, together with a colleague, to assess your leadership skills.

Some of the Activities may provide the basis of evidence for your S/NVQ portfolio. All Portfolio Activities and the Work-based assignment are signposted with this icon.

The icon states the elements to which the portfolio activities and Work-based assignment relate.

The Work-based assignment (on page 76) involves gathering views about your leadership qualities and skills from a number of people. It is designed to help you meet element C1.1 of the Management Standards: 'Develop your own skills to improve your performance' and the personal competence: 'Managing self – managing personal learning and development'. You may want to prepare for it in advance.

Session A
Are you a leader?

 **I Introduction**

> 'For leadership is not magnetic personality – that can just as well be demagoguery. It is not "making friends and influencing people" – that is salesmanship. Leadership is the lifting of a man's vision to higher sights, the raising of a man's performance to a higher standard, the building of a man's personality beyond its normal limitations. Nothing better prepares the ground for such leadership than a spirit of management that confirms in the day-to-day practices of the organization strict principles of conduct and responsibility, high standards of performance, and respect for the individual and his work.'
>
> Peter F. Drucker, *The Practice of Management*[2]

Peter Drucker's words, written in 1955, apply to team leaders in all walks of life, and of course to women as well as men.

Some leaders are tall and muscular; others are small and petite. One leader may be outgoing and jolly, while another always looks serious. All leaders have their own individual personalities, styles and approaches to the task. Identifying the characteristics of leadership is not easy.

But there are many qualities that all leaders have and need. In this session of the workbook we'll be looking at what those qualities are. We'll be asking whether leadership can really be learned. And we'll try to determine what a good leader should be and what a good leader should do.

---

[2] Peter F. Drucker (1989), *The Practice of Management*, Butterworth-Heinemann.

2 What is a leader?

An overheard conversation:

'Leaders are born with special qualities. Some people stand out from the crowd. You've either got it or you haven't.'

'Nonsense. Anyone can become a leader. It's a skill and can be learned like any other.'

Activity 1

4 mins

Do you agree with either of these arguments? Give a brief reason for your answer.

_____

_____

_____

EXTENSION 1
John Adair's excellent book *Effective Leadership* is intended to be a self-development manual for leaders and potential leaders.

There are arguments to be made for both sides. Throughout history there have been remarkable leaders, who seem to have had 'charisma' – the ability to inspire followers with devotion and enthusiasm. Some examples that come to mind are listed below, in no particular order.

Mahatma Gandhi (1869–1948) the Indian nationalist leader, trained as a lawyer and, having spent twenty years in South Africa fighting for better treatment of Indians there, returned to his native country, leading the campaign for home rule.

Nelson Mandela (born 1918) was also a lawyer, and the son of a tribal chief. He became South Africa's first non-white president, despite having been imprisoned for sabotage and treason from 1964 to 1990.

Emmeline Pankhurst (1858–1928) the suffragette, was educated in Manchester and Paris and led the movement to win the vote for British women, whose aims were eventually achieved a few weeks before she died.

Golda Meir (1898–1978) was an Israeli prime minister, and one of the founders of the State of Israel. She was born in Russia (the Ukraine), emigrated to the USA and trained as a teacher, before becoming active in the Zionist movement.

George Washington (1732–99), despite having had virtually no formal schooling, became commander-in-chief of the Continental army during the American Revolution, and later the first president of the United States.

Sir Winston Churchill (1874–1965) had a privileged background – as the son of a Lord – and was probably the best-loved and most famous British leader in the last century. In his early life he had trained as a soldier.

Each of these made a significant mark on history. To their followers they were heroes or heroines. In each case there was also opposition to these leaders. Great leaders do not necessarily use their abilities to achieve good ends – notable examples of leaders who used their abilities to evil effect are Hitler and Stalin.

You may agree that most leaders are not born with special qualities, but learn leadership. The leaders of industry and commerce usually fall into this category. Typically, leaders start out in junior positions and learn the skills of leadership as they progress.

In this workbook we are mainly interested in leadership in organizations, where people tend to connect the words 'manager' and 'leader'. But are they the same thing?

2.1 Are leaders managers?

It's part of the job of managers to lead, even though some of them may not seem to do it very well! But does a leader necessarily manage?

To answer this question, we need to consider what the job of a manager consists of. The first difficulty we face is the fact that the role of managers in organizations is changing. Viewed in traditional terms, a manager has to:

- **plan**

  decide what has to be done, and when, where and how it is to be done;

- **organize and co-ordinate**

  harmonize the efforts of the people engaged in the enterprise;

- **monitor and control**

  ensure that what the manager wants to happen really is happening, and do something about it if it isn't;

- **communicate**

  convey information to others, and be receptive to feedback;

- **support and motivate**

  others in their efforts;

- **evaluate**

  appraise the performance of others and assess results.

Certainly most leaders at work do all these things, although a leader at the top of an organization may place much more emphasis on planning and evaluating results than, say, organizing and co-ordinating.

Nowadays, however, the work of a manager is just as likely to consist of:

- **coaching** others;
- **empowering** individuals and teams to organize and control their own work;
- **creating an environment** in which employees are encouraged to find out what needs doing, and then get on with it;
- **building trust**;
- **focusing on the customer's needs**;
- **exploring ways to improve performance**;
- **breaking down barriers** to change and growth.

EXTENSION 2
'Traditional manager/ employee roles are changing in . . . areas like decision making and problem solving where the necessary authority and autonomy has been effectively delegated to teams and individuals, leaving them empowered to think for themselves. To achieve this many managers have had to fundamentally alter their own approach to become less directive, more guiding and more enabling.'
Teambuilding by John Adair.

But whichever set of management functions we assume, does this get us any nearer to defining what a leader is? You may know someone who is able to attract a following, even though his or her managing skills may leave much to be desired. And you may know a competent manager who seems unable to inspire others – who has no 'personal magnetism'.

A leader has to have followers, and to get people to follow you, it's necessary to persuade and influence them: to guide their actions and opinions. Some managers are better at this than others.

In summary we can say that the functions of management do not entirely coincide with the qualities required of leadership. As Andrzej Huczynski and David Buchanan say in their book *Organizational Behaviour*:

> The functions of leaders are not the same as the functions of management. In some respects they are separate and in others they overlap.

2.2 Team leaders

EXTENSION 3
Further details about
Organizational Behaviour
can be found on page 86.

Although managers are usually expected to lead teams, it is possible to carry out many management functions, and yet not be expected (or necessarily be able) to lead others. However, many managers will be expected to lead teams of people as part of their management role. A team leader, on the other hand, may not have the title of manager nor carry out many of the key activities that go with being a manager. So, to summarise, some managers may lead teams, but people who are just team leaders will not have the responsibilities that go with being a manager. This table shows how the two roles (generally) compare.

A Team Leader	A Manager
■ leads a group of individuals, working to a common purpose ■ works towards achieving the team's (shorter term) objectives ■ focuses the team on achieving its goals ■ sets clear roles and responsibilities for each team member ■ needs to be able to adapt quickly to changing circumstances	■ manages a more diverse range of processes, using a variety of resources ■ works towards to achieving the organization's (longer term) objectives ■ organises and co-ordinates activity over a wide range of functions ■ allocates work to individuals, whose responsibilities can vary over time ■ plans and implements change over time

The key differences between a team leader and a manager are that:

■ a team leader is likely to be working within clearly prescribed and limited timescales, while a manager can take a longer-term view of their area of responsibility

■ a team leader has responsibility only for the team, a manager may have responsibility for people in more than one team.

2.3 What qualities does a leader need?

So how can we identify the characteristics of effective leadership? If we think about the enormous range of situations in which leaders are found, it is difficult to see how it is possible to sum up what makes a good leader in a few words. Take these three cases, for example.

Frank was a passenger on a ship that hit a freighter and started to sink. Many people on board panicked, but Frank kept calm and helped the crew organize lifeboats. Then he took the lead in getting other passengers to safety. When they all got to dry land, Frank was praised for his presence of mind and leadership qualities.

Marek was a team leader of aircraft mechanics in his country's air force. During an emergency operation, it was the job of Marek's team to keep the aircraft flying. This involved long, painstaking work under trying conditions. A single mistake could have caused an aeroplane to crash, which would have jeopardized the whole mission. When the operation was over, Marek's commanding officer congratulated him on his devotion to duty and remarkable leadership.

Bettina led a team of computer operators, that had worked away steadily for several years in a large company. The quality of the team's work was consistently high, staff turnover low and the team the envy of many other first line managers. Bettina's leadership qualities were recognized and, when a vacancy arose, she got promoted to departmental manager.

It's easy to spot the **differences** between the three cases.

■ Frank, unlike the other two, wasn't even an appointed leader and yet took charge when an emergency situation arose.
■ Both Marek and Bettina led a team; Marek had to inspire his mechanics to put in a supreme effort during a limited exercise.
■ In Bettina's case, although conditions weren't particularly arduous, she set herself the task of maintaining very high team standards over a long period.

But what about the **similarities**?

Activity 2 · 5 mins

What characteristics were common to the three leaders above? Jot down **two** or **three** features that apply to all three cases.

_____

_____

_____

_____

_____

You may have noted that all three leaders must have had the following qualities.

■ **The ability to influence others**.

They each had to persuade other people to follow their lead. Tact, diplomacy and other 'people skills' were required. At times this may have meant, especially for Frank, having to be polite yet firm in getting people to do what was wanted.

■ **The ability to inspire confidence**

by setting an example and/or imposing high standards.

■ **Managing skills**,

> To be a leader, you need more than managing skills.

including the ability to organize and co-ordinate, to communicate well and to support and motivate.

■ **Sound personal qualities**

for others to believe in them and want to follow them.

■ **Determination**

in abundance.

Judging by our interpretation of these cases, it appears that managing skills are only one aspect of leadership. All the others are just as important.

Activity 3

Read the above list again. Are there any other characteristics displayed by effective leaders, that we haven't mentioned? Think of the day-to-day running of a workteam, or think instead of any leader you particularly respect and admire. What other qualities does a **team** look for in a team leader? Try to list **two** points.

_____

_____

_____

You may have included such leadership characteristics as:

- **dependability**

  never letting the team down;

- **integrity**

  being uncompromising in keeping to a set of values;

- **fairness**

  not taking sides, but being even-handed;

- **being a good listener**

  rather than always trying to dominate discussions;

- **consistency**

  not changing values or rules to suit the circumstances;

- **having a genuine interest in others**

  liking people and identifying with them,

- **showing confidence in the team**

  being prepared to hand over power, authority and responsibility to the team;

- **giving credit where it's due**

  rather than claiming all the credit for the leader;

- **standing by the team when it's in trouble**

  and not trying to disclaim responsibility for the problems;

■ **keeping the team informed**

and not hiding behind a 'cloak of mystery'.

Generally, too, good leaders have a **history of success and achievement**.

This is now quite a list. Let's set out these points again, to remind ourselves what we've covered so far.

Leaders have:	A good leader will:
■ **the ability to inspire confidence** ■ **managing skills** ■ **sound personal qualities** ■ **determination** ■ **dependability** ■ **integrity** ■ **a history of success and achievement.**	■ **be fair** ■ **be a good listener** ■ **be consistent** ■ **have a genuine interest in others** ■ **show confidence in the team** ■ **give credit where it's due** ■ **stand by the team when it's in trouble** ■ **keep the team informed.**

Of course, it doesn't mean to say that all leaders are strong in all these areas. History has shown that leaders may have many weaknesses, often including an unwarranted confidence in their own abilities!

In summary, we can separate the skills and qualities of an effective leader into four groups.

■ **People skills**.
■ **Personal qualities**.
■ **Managing skills**.
■ **Personal achievements**.

The following diagram illustrates this.

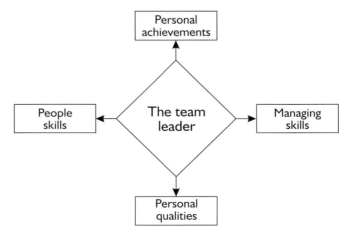

2.4 Can leadership be learned?

Activity 4 · ⏱ 8 mins

Categorize the leadership qualities we have listed into the four groups, and then indicate which of them you think can be learned or acquired. (Some of the qualities may well fit into more than one of the four groups.) Tick the relevant boxes.

	People skills	Personal qualities	Managing skills	Personal achievements	Can be learned
The ability to inspire confidence	☐	☐	☐	☐	☐
Determination	☐	☐	☐	☐	☐
Dependability	☐	☐	☐	☐	☐
Integrity	☐	☐	☐	☐	☐
A history of success and achievement	☐	☐	☐	☐	☐
Fairness	☐	☐	☐	☐	☐
Listening skills	☐	☐	☐	☐	☐
Consistency	☐	☐	☐	☐	☐
A genuine interest in others	☐	☐	☐	☐	☐
Displaying confidence in the team	☐	☐	☐	☐	☐
Giving credit where it's due	☐	☐	☐	☐	☐
The willingness to stand by the team	☐	☐	☐	☐	☐
Being good at keeping the team informed	☐	☐	☐	☐	☐

Answers can be found on pages 90–1.

You will notice that in the suggested answer that there's a tick against everything in the 'Can be learned' column, except for 'determination' and 'a genuine interest in others'.

In a sense, these two qualities are the starting points for leadership. Perhaps you will agree that anyone who doesn't have determination, or who isn't interested in people, may do better to set aside his or her ambitions to become a leader.

> Determination is essential, because all leaders have to overcome difficulties and obstacles, as our three case studies illustrated.

> It is true that there have been autocratic leaders who have been much more interested in themselves and their own ambitions, than in the people they led. But you have to be a very forceful person to get away with this! Unless you intend becoming a dictator, an interest in people is a pre-requisite for leadership.

To be a leader, you need determination to succeed, and to like working with people.

You may have found it surprising that other personal qualities like dependability and integrity can be learned. Perhaps you don't believe it. After all, there are few training schools with 'fairness' or 'consistency' on the curriculum. These kinds of attributes might be considered part of a person's character – you are either dependable or you aren't, for instance.

But there's more to it than this. Often, it is not until people are put into situations where others depend upon them that they display such qualities. And many would argue that these 'personal competences' **can** be learned, or at least developed, although it may take much longer to develop some than others.

Let's review them. First, we should define some of these personal qualities.

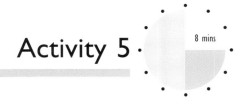

Activity 5

8 mins

Give an example of what you mean when you say someone:

■ is dependable _____

_____

_____

_____

■ has integrity _____

_____

_____

_____

■ is fair _____

_____

_____

_____

■ is consistent _____

_____

_____

_____

See whether you agree with the following.

■ **Dependable** people are reliable.

They can be confidently trusted to do and say what they say they will. A dependable leader who promises to reward the team will do so. Dependable people are there when you need them.

You could probably think of many examples of people learning to be dependable. Many of us were not very reliable in our youth, because adolescence is a time when people are changing fast; we learn to be dependable as we grow up and take on more responsibilities. Often, people aren't dependable until they are expected to be. For example, new parents learn very quickly that they must always be there for the child: there is no escape from this responsibility. Team members, too, may often appear to be unreliable until the leader puts his or her complete faith in them. You might say that

people tend to be dependable when others expect them to be.

■ **Integrity** is honesty and uprightness, or an adherence to moral principles.

Leaders who have integrity don't cheat and will stick to their ideals. If there is one quality that a leader gets respected for, this is it.

Although it is perhaps not helpful to talk about 'learning to have integrity', most of us are capable (most of the time!) of behaving with honesty. In fact

to get the respect of a team, you need to be honest with them, and show you care about certain ideals.

■ To behave **fairly**, you have to be just and unbiased in your treatment of people.

Perceived unfairness is often the cause of discontent in teams.

It is difficult to be fair in all your dealings with others. The main thing is to **want** to be fair – and that doesn't take much learning.

Few of us are always fair. All that others can expect of you is that you try very hard to be fair.

■ In one sense, **consistency** is very close to integrity.

It also means being steadfast and unchanging: not altering your mind at every new suggestion or setback.

In the managerial sense, being consistent has a great deal to do with decision-making. For a person who tends to be undecided between different courses or opinions, it can be hard to learn to be consistent.

Decision-making is the following process.

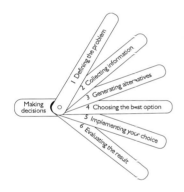

1 Defining the problem.
2 Collecting information.
3 Generating alternatives.
4 Choosing the best option.
5 Implementing your choice.
6 Evaluating the result.

Inconsistent decision makers may **appear** to waver between steps 4 and 5. **In fact**, what usually happens is that they don't spend enough time and effort on steps 1 and 2.

To be consistent in your decision-making, be clear in your mind about the problem, and then collect facts and opinions before you decide.

So, in summary, we have identified a number of leadership qualities, and shown that these qualities can all – or nearly all – be learned or acquired.

But are there any other attributes that a leader must have?

3 What else does a leader need?

3.1 A desire for the job

Read the following account and then note down what you think about it.

Activity 6 · 8 mins

Milly Covacic was a trained laboratory technician and had been doing the same kind of work for five years, since she left college. She was employed in a large chemical company and Milly was respected by others in the department for her professional skills. She was naturally a quiet person, but she was pleasant enough, and enjoyed her job.

One day the workteam supervisor left and Milly was offered the post. She didn't give it much thought, and, because the money was better, she accepted straight away.

When she started her new job, Milly found it very hard not to carry on working in the same way she had before. She knew it was up to her to lead the rest of the team, but whenever she saw someone doing a job badly she took over the work herself – it was easier than trying to get other members of the team to do it better. When the department manager found out what was going on, she wasn't at all pleased. 'You have to ask yourself whether you really want to be a team leader, Milly, or a technician. If you are in charge, you can't carry on in the same way as before.'

Milly has to ask herself some searching questions. Suggest **two** things she should be deciding in her own mind.

_____

_____

_____

How you respond to this activity will depend upon what kind person you are. A decision has to be made, nevertheless. Milly must ask herself what she wants.

■ Does she really want to be a team leader?
■ Has she the necessary ambition and desire, apart from wanting the extra money?
■ Does she have the confidence in herself to tackle the job?

If she does, she has to learn to act like a leader. This means a complete rethink of her approach to the job. She might reasonably ask her manager for training and advice.

To lead a team you must have a real commitment to the role, and must have belief in yourself to lead others. This is the most basic qualification for becoming a leader.

To be a leader you have to want to be one and believe in your own ability to be one.

3.2 Do you need to be an expert?

Milly does start with one important advantage, which will help her in her new role. She is a skilled technician, which means she will know the work of the other technicians well. She will be able to help them and guide them, though we would hope not to the extent of taking over their work!

More importantly, she will be able to **spot quickly when things are going wrong**.

She will be respected for her knowledge, which will give her more authority.

To lead others, it helps to be experienced in the work they do.

But many leaders find themselves in the position of having less expertise than others in the team; does it matter?

The answer is no, but it does raise problems.

Activity 7 · 5 mins

What difficulties may be encountered by someone who has to lead a team of specialists, and who therefore has less expertise in certain areas than other members of the team? Try to jot down **two** possible difficulties.

_____

_____

_____

_____

The difficulties may be expressed as questions that the leader might ask, such as:

> 'How can I be sure that what they are telling me is correct?'
> 'How can I assess their performance?'
> 'How can I monitor and understand what is going on?'

or perhaps:

> 'How can I avoid looking foolish and ignorant, faced with all this expert knowledge?'

It's perfectly possible for a 'layperson' to lead a team of specialists: it happens all the time. However, it is important to recognize the possible problems, and to make provisions for dealing with them.

Most difficulties may be overcome once there is trust. A team member who has shown his or her abilities, and is not in the habit of setting out to deceive, can be trusted to impart correct and reliable information. The leader may have to ask that the knowledge be given in a condensed form, using non-technical language. What can be a mistake is for the leader to take no interest in the work of a specialist, for fear of looking foolish. We can't all be experts in everything, but most technical information can be put in a form that the non-expert can understand.

The best and easiest way of assessing performance is by results.

- The software engineer's work will be judged by the users of the programs written.
- The doctor's work is evaluated by his or her record on treating patients.
- Most of all, the work of the team's members is judged by the results achieved by the team.

To summarize, we can say that, although it **helps** to have as much expertise as your team, it isn't necessary. When leading teams with specialists:

You don't have to know everything your team members do.

- try to build up trust;
- don't be afraid to question;
- get synopses and explanations in non-expert language;
- judge by results;
- if necessary, cross-check performance and information with other experts.

4 So how do you become an effective leader?

There are many kinds of leader, as the ability to lead has little to do with physical characteristics, educational or family background, or personality. However, what **does** seem to be important is that leaders set their own **standards**.

As we have discussed, most of the attributes of leadership can be learned. With practice and determination, you can even learn to be fair and dependable and consistent. But how? It doesn't seem easy to acquire the qualities of leadership.

Thinking about the famous leaders listed earlier, you may have noted that many were driven by very strong beliefs. Emmeline Pankhurst fervently believed that women should have equal voting rights with men; Gandhi felt compelled to act to defend his fellow Indians against oppression through 'truth and firmness'; Golda Meir was dedicated to Jewish nationalism. We can easily imagine how the behaviour of these leaders would be dictated by their passionate convictions, and that their single-mindedness would draw followers to each cause.

So in great leaders, it seems, standards of behaviour are often the result of devotion to an ideal or belief. For us ordinary mortals, doing ordinary jobs, life isn't usually like that. Nevertheless, in commerce and industry, just as in other fields of human endeavour,

the way that a leader's behaviour is viewed by others will largely determine how successful the leader is.

In many organizations, standards of behaviour are made clear: people know what is expected of them, because there is a corporate 'ethic' which implies a certain code of conduct. To repeat the words of Peter Drucker from our quotation in the introduction to this session:

> Nothing better prepares the ground for such leadership than a spirit of management that confirms in the day-to-day practices of the organization strict principles of conduct and responsibility, high standards of performance, and respect for the individual and his work.'

In such a culture, there will typically be many role models for the aspiring leader to follow. The corporate standards reinforce the team leader's message, and provide a strong incentive for the team. The leader still has plenty to do – setting team objectives, communicating, motivating, and so on – but the job is made easier, because team members know the whole company is behind them.

In a poorly run organization, however, the leader who tries to set his or her own high standards may seem to face an uphill struggle. But the job still has to be done.

Whatever kind of organization you work in, you may find the following advice useful.

■ **Find a role model**

if you can – someone you respect highly. Ask yourself what it is you admire about this leader, and aim to reach his or her standards of behaviour. If you can find a mentor – an experienced person to act as your adviser – that would be even better.

■ **Be yourself**

Even if you decide to model yourself on another leader, don't try to copy: do things in your own way, but to the same high standards.

■ **Keep your objectives clearly in mind**

including your personal aims and ambitions. By training your sights on your end-goals, you won't be so easily put off by problems along the way.

■ **Know your strengths and weaknesses**

Remember that few leaders have the ideal qualifications for the job, but the more determined ones win through in spite of their shortcomings.

■ **Stick to your principles**

You will recall the point made earlier: if there is one quality that earns respect, it is integrity.

Stephen worked in petrochemical engineering. When first appointed to team leader, Stephen was regarded as something of a joke. He had a speech defect which made him stammer, and was not physically strong. He looked nervous and vulnerable. But, as his team gradually found out, Stephen was wise, open, and above all, steadfast in adversity. He never let his team down, and he always adhered to the principles he believed in, without ever becoming stubborn. Stephen was very able, too, and finished up running the company.

Activity 8

15 mins

Use the following questions as prompts to help you decide the actions you intend to take in order to become a more effective leader.

Who are the leaders you most admire?

_____

_____

_____

_____

What are the qualities you most respect in them?

_____

_____

_____

_____

Who, if anyone, could act as your mentor?

_____

_____

_____

_____

What are your personal objectives, so far as leadership is concerned?

_____

_____

_____

_____

Review the following list of leadership qualities, and say how strong you think you are in each of them, by ticking the appropriate box.

You:	Strong	Fairly strong	Fairly weak	Weak
■ stick to certain principles;	☐	☐	☐	☐
■ have clear objectives;	☐	☐	☐	☐
■ are consistent;	☐	☐	☐	☐
■ have good communication skills;	☐	☐	☐	☐
■ try to treat people fairly;	☐	☐	☐	☐
■ are dependable;	☐	☐	☐	☐
■ like people;	☐	☐	☐	☐
■ are always willing to stand by the team;	☐	☐	☐	☐
■ are determined to become a more effective leader.	☐	☐	☐	☐

Now explain what action you intend to take to overcome your weaknesses.

_____

_____

_____

_____

_____

You may want to look back at your response to this activity when you attempt the Work-based assignment on page 76.

Self-assessment 1

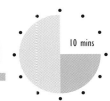

10 mins

Complete the following sentences with a suitable word or words chosen from the list below.

1   To be a leader, you need _____ to succeed, and to like working with _____.

2   People tend to be _____ when others _____ them to be.

3   To get the _____ of a team, you need to be honest with them, and show you care about certain _____.

4   Few of us are always _____. All that others can expect of you is that you try very hard to be fair.

5   To be _____ in your decision-making, be clear in your mind about the problem, and then collect _____ and _____ before you decide.

6   To _____ others, it helps to be _____ in the work they do.

7   The way that a leader's _____ is viewed by others will largely determine how _____ the leader is.

CONSISTENT	EXPERIENCED	OPINIONS
BEHAVIOUR	FACTS	PEOPLE
DEPENDABLE	FAIR	RESPECT
DETERMINATION	IDEALS	SUCCESSFUL
EXPECT	LEAD	

8   Fill in the blanks in the following diagram, showing the four groups of skills and qualities that an effective leader requires.

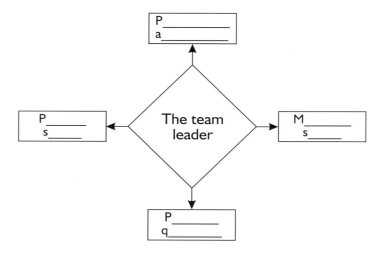

9   Which **six** of the following ten characteristics are recognized as being important in good leadership?

    dependability
    height
    ability to listen
    good communication skills
    integrity
    an extrovert personality
    high intelligence
    ability to inspire confidence
    methodical approach
    good managing skills.

Answers to these questions can be found on pages 87–8.

5 Summary

- Leaders are not necessarily managers, although most leaders working for organizations will have managerial skills. The functions of leaders are not the same as the functions of management. In some respects they are separate and in others they overlap.

- A leader has to have followers, and to get people to follow you, it's necessary to persuade and influence them: to guide their actions and opinions.

- Leaders have:
  - the ability to inspire confidence
  - managing skills
  - sound personal qualities
  - determination
  - dependability
  - integrity
  - a history of success and achievement.

- A good leader will:
  - be fair
  - be a good listener
  - be consistent
  - have a genuine interest in others
  - show confidence in the team
  - give credit where it's due
  - stand by the team when it's in trouble
  - keep the team informed.

- In summary, we can separate the skills and qualities of an effective leader into four groups:
  - people skills
  - personal qualities
  - managing skills
  - personal achievements.

- To be a leader, you need determination to succeed, and to like working with people.

- People tend to be dependable when others expect them to be.

- To get the respect of a team, you need to be honest with them, and show you care about certain ideals.

- Few of us are always fair. All that others can expect of you is that you try very hard to be fair.

- To be consistent in your decision-making, be clear in your mind about the problem, and then collect facts and opinions before you decide.

- To be a leader you have to want to be one and believe in your own ability to be one.

- To lead others, it helps to be experienced in the work they do.

- The way that leaders' behaviour is perceived will largely determine how successful they are.

Session B
The team leader – responsibilities and roles

1 Introduction

> 'My own conviction is that every leader should have enough humility to accept, publicly, the responsibility for the mistakes of the subordinates he has himself selected and, likewise, to give them credit, publicly, for their triumphs. I am aware that some popular theories of leadership hold that the top man must always keep his "image" bright and shining. I believe, however, that in the long run fairness and honesty, and a generous attitude towards subordinates and associates, pay off.'
>
> Dwight David Eisenhower, Allied Supreme Commander during World War II, and 34th president of the United States.[3]

A lot is expected of a team leader. If you have already led a team you will know that people look to you to be both resourceful and independent. The team demands your loyalty and so does the organization. When things aren't going well, you must still take the responsibility, and when the team succeeds, it is the team members who should get the praise.

But the job has its compensations. Being a team leader is nearly always challenging and often very rewarding. It is seldom boring!

In this session of the workbook we start by looking at responsibilities of the team leader, which can be identified in terms of three points of view: the task, the individual and the team. We then investigate the difficulties and confusion that can result from the various roles played by team leaders and team members, and how to deal with them.

---

[3] Quoted in *Effective Leadership* (Extension 1).

2 Responsibility 1: the task

EXTENSION 1
The Adair book is listed on page 82.

John Adair, in his book *Effective Leadership*, uses a three-circle model to represent the triple responsibilities of the team and team leader.

Which of these is the most important?

Activity 9

8 mins

Read this account of a supervisor's interview with her line manager, and then say what you think about it.

Hannah wasn't happy. She had taken over as team leader of a team of process operators in a company making small assemblies, nine months before. She thought she had been doing well, but was rather disappointed in the annual merit pay rise she had received. Hannah asked to see her manager and said to him: 'When I took over this team, morale was low, things were badly organized and most of the people on the team were not properly trained for the jobs they were doing.'

Hannah then went on to give an account of all the work she had done to improve things since she had taken over the running of the team. Hannah's manager heard her out patiently, and then said:

'It's true that you have done very well, Hannah, and I agree with what you say. However, the fact remains that the output and quality of your team's work is still below the others. We want people to be happy and trained and well motivated. All these things are important. But you musn't forget that your team has been set up in order to help us manufacture high quality goods at an economic rate.'

From what you've read of the case, do you think Hannah's manager is justified in criticizing her in this way? Jot down your views.

_____

_____

_____

_____

_____

Without knowing any more about the details, I think I'd broadly agree with the points made by Hannah's manager. Achievement of the main task is the team leader's prime responsibility, because **the allotted task is the reason for the workteam's existence: all other considerations are secondary**.

Management will look to the team leader to ensure that the team's task is accomplished. And the team will look to the team leader to guide them through the difficulties of achieving the task.

Achievement of the task is the team leader's main responsibility.

Of course, there are other responsibilities, as we've already hinted. Not least among these is a **responsibility towards individuals**.

3 Responsibility 2: the individual

What does 'responsibility towards individuals' mean, do you think?

Activity 10

8 mins

Read the following account, and jot down any points which it suggests to you about the responsibilities of the team leader towards the individuals in a team.

John Spicer was a social worker, employed by a local authority. When John's new team leader, Mary Harrison, was appointed, John was glad of the opportunity to have a long chat with her. Mary had encouraged John to speak freely about his problems. Here's an extract of what John had to say:

'Before you came, Mary, we were left very much to our own devices. We got very little support and not much encouragement. As you know, this job can be very tough at times. I've been physically attacked on a couple of occasions, for instance, by the very people I was trying to help. Also, I know people in the team who have been given jobs which they had no training or preparation for. What's more, there isn't any proper system of reviewing objectives or performance, so we don't know how well we've been doing or what is expected of us.'

You may have noticed that John made several points which remind us about the responsibility of team leaders towards individuals. These include:

- **supporting and encouraging the individual;**
- **assigning tasks appropriate to the member's abilities;**
- **making clear the job roles of the team members;**
- **assessing performance;**
- (if necessary) **protecting the individual** from other people, including other members of the group.

These are important points, so let's go through each one in turn.

3.1 Supporting and encouraging the individual

One of the best parts of belonging to a team is that you aren't on your own. In the best teams, each member can look to the others for assistance and encouragement. In particular, the team leader is ready and able to provide help, guidance and support.

This has more to do with adopting a positive and sharing approach than with any kind of management technique. You could ask yourself the following questions.

- 'Do I make myself available when team members need me?'
- 'Do I give recognition to individual effort and achievement?'
- 'Do I praise loudly and criticize quietly?'
- 'Do I encourage everyone to make a full contribution to the team?'

3.2 Assigning appropriate tasks

When we talk about 'assigning tasks that are appropriate to the team member's abilities', we **don't** mean:

- tasks that are too easy:

    as easy tasks lead to boredom. Bored people make mistakes, and become frustrated through not being able to use their full range of skills and abilities.

- tasks that are too difficult:

    for people faced with tasks they can't manage become unhappy and lose confidence.

The ideal task will stretch an individual, and give a feeling of exhilaration and triumph when success has been achieved.

Matching the tasks to be performed with the capabilities of each person may require a lot of time and thought on the part of the leader. Even though perfect matching may seldom be realized, it shouldn't stop us striving for the ideal.

There are lots of ways of matching.

- If a task is too difficult for team member A, and too easy for team member B, why not get them to work together? Next time, A may be able to manage it with less help. You will have helped A develop, and given B a training and supporting role, which can be challenging and interesting in itself.
- You may find ways of making a task more demanding by, for example, setting higher targets of quality, or reducing the permitted time for completion.

■ You might discover ways of making a task less demanding by, for example, breaking it down into smaller sub-tasks.

■ Gaps between the abilities of individuals and the expertise required to finish a task, may be bridged by training, either on or off the job.

3.3 Clarifying job roles

As we will discuss later, role conflict and ambiguity is a common complaint, which can result in serious problems.

'Who am I? Where do I fit in? What am I supposed to be doing? In which direction am I heading?' All these questions will be asked by the team member who isn't clear about his or her role in the team. (Unfortunately, such questions are not always asked explicitly or expressed out loud.)

Work not getting done is a common symptom of uncertainty over job roles. When a task is apparently ignored or postponed without reason, the leader may have to make plain what needs to be done, who should be doing it, and (if necessary) how, when and where it should be done.

3.4 Assessing performance

Assessment is typically a key task for a team leader. Try the next activity, to see how well you match up at the moment.

Activity 11

12 mins

S/NVQ C12.2

This Activity may provide the basis of appropriate evidence for your S/NVQ portfolio. If you are intending to take this course of action, it might be better to write your answers on separate sheets of paper.

Explain the steps you take, or plan to take, to ensure the following.

■ You communicate the purpose of assessment to everyone involved.

_____

_____

_____

_____

■ You give your team opportunities to assess their own work.

_____

_____

_____

_____

■ Assessment of work takes place at the best times, when it is most likely to maintain and improve effective performance.

_____

_____

_____

_____

■ Assessments are based on evidence that is sufficiently valid and reliable.

_____

_____

_____

_____

■ Assessments are carried out objectively, against criteria that are clear and agreed.

_____

_____

_____

_____

Your response to this Activity will depend on your own job and organization, and also on your individual approach to leadership. There are no strict rules about these things; we all have our own style and methods.

The idea of getting the team to assess its own performance may be new to you. The purpose is to encourage each person to assess his or her own performance and the performance of the team as a whole. Here is a list of some suitable prompting questions.

■ 'Did you/we reach the task objectives?'
■ 'If not, why not: what were the precise reasons for failure? What would you do differently next time? Are the objectives themselves unrealistic?'

- 'If the task was successfully accomplished, what do you think you/we learned? What can we apply to other tasks? Should we set higher targets?'
- 'How well did we work as a team?'
- 'How could we do things better?'

3.5 Protecting the individual

Individuals may need protection from other team members, from other teams, from outside interference – or perhaps from themselves!

It's easy to conjure up an image of a mother hen protecting her chicks, but this analogy is perhaps a little off the mark. People at work are adults, and shouldn't need much protection, most of the time.

However, some people and some occupations are more vulnerable to manipulation, bullying and other forms of pressure than others. In an earlier activity, John Spicer gave an account of physical attacks on staff. Social workers, teachers, police officers and those in other professions may be subject to such abuse, and may have to depend on limited systems of security to protect them. Team leaders have to do what they can to ensure that security measures are adequate for local conditions.

Forms of protection from other kinds of pressure may include:

- clamping down on verbal abuse;
- breaking up exclusive cliques;
- defending team members against outside criticism;
- encouraging more experienced members to give help and advice to those who are finding their feet.

The third responsibility of the team leader is towards **the team as a whole**.

4 Responsibility 3: the team

The team is made up of people and yet it also has an identity of its own.

Activity 12

5 mins

Apart from the responsibilities towards individuals that we listed above, what are the leader's responsibilities towards the team as a whole?

One example is 'demonstrating a total commitment to the task and the team'. Try to list **three** other points.

_____

_____

_____

_____

You may agree that the team leader is responsible for:

- **demonstrating a commitment** to the team;
- **setting out and agreeing the overall and specific aims and objectives**, so that everyone knows what has to be done and why it has to be done;
- **helping to ensure that the standards of the group are maintained**;
- **supporting the team when things are going against it**.

Yet another set of responsibilities concerns the relationship of the team to other groups. The team leader is also normally charged with:

- **representing the team to management**;
- **representing management to the team**;
- **co-ordinating with other teams and departments**.

This can be shown in the form of a diagram:

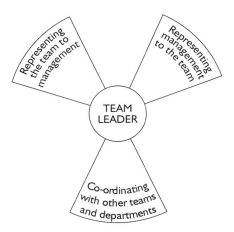

What does this mean exactly?

We can think of the leader as a hub: a central point of interest and activity. At one spoke of the wheel is the team, and at a second are the other levels of organizational management. A third spoke symbolizes other teams and people, typically including the team's direct customers and suppliers.

To say that 'the leader represents management to the team' means the following.

When the team members think of the organization's management, they think first of the team leader. For, so far as they are concerned, it is the leader who is empowered to interpret higher management's demands and wishes.	If the team want to communicate with 'the powers that be', they will normally expect to do so through the leader, for he or she is their representative. (However, this does not of course mean to say that all communications must go through the leader.)

When we say 'the leader represents the team to management' we are implying that:

- the team leader's success or failure is largely dependent on the fortunes of the team;
- if higher management wish to communicate with the team, they will do so via the leader, as their representative.

In a similar fashion, the leader represents, and is a representative of, the team, in the eyes of all others, inside or outside the organization.

After all this, you may be wondering how you can cope with these various responsibilities and roles.

5 Coping with the role of team leader

5.1 Role ambiguity

If you aren't certain about some aspect of the role you are meant to be playing, you may well become confused and inefficient.

To take a simple illustration, suppose your manager tells you she is unhappy about the amount of litter in the car park and tells you to 'sort it out'.

What are you meant to do?

- Act in the role of hygienist, and get the litter picked up?
- Act in the role of disciplinarian and reprimand the people who drop litter?
- Act as liaison officer and report the matter to Security?

Of course, a situation like this would only cause you temporary uncertainty. However, if you are generally unsure of your role at work the consequences might be more damaging – to you, to the organization or both.

We can call uncertainty about roles **role ambiguity**.

As a team leader, it is largely up to you to define the job-related roles of team members and to try to ensure that role ambiguity is dealt with as far as you can.

But what about your own role?

'Role ambiguity results when there is some uncertainty in the minds, either of the focal person or of the members of his role set, as to precisely what his role is at any given time.'
Charles B. Handy (1993), *Understanding Organizations* Penguin.

Activity 13 · 3 mins

One example of role ambiguity is being unsure about what is expected of you in terms of performance; perhaps your manager didn't make clear the standard of work required.

Have you ever been uncertain about any aspect of your role or position at work? If so, answer the following questions briefly.

What form did your own role uncertainty take?

_____

_____

_____

What did you do about it?

_____

_____

_____

For example, you may have had an experience of uncertainty about your:

■ **responsibility**

being uncertain about just what your responsibilities were in a certain situation – say, one day when you were left in charge without specific instructions;

■ **expected work performance**

working for someone who wasn't consistent about the standards demanded of you or the method of assessment to be used;

■ **scope for advancement**

not knowing how you can move forward from where you are.

Situations like this are common, and should be regarded as challenges.

There is a drive among many organizations these days to devolve responsibility downwards, through continuous improvement programmes, self-managed teams, multi-skilling, empowerment and so on. If any of these changes are taking place where you work, it probably means that your role as team leader is becoming more ambiguous. You may act as spokesperson for the group but not have much in the way of authority; in this case, you are more of a **facilitator** than a leader.

Parts of the organization may operate in a non-standard way; an example is the setting up of autonomous work cells in an otherwise traditionally managed factory. You may have to report to more than one manager, or lead more than one team. Most managers are required to take on different roles from time to time. Wherever change and experimentation is going on, there is likely to be role ambiguity.

Role ambiguity is part of the experience of being a manager.

5.2 Role conflict and role incompatibility

Imagine holding a meeting of your workteam, where you are playing the role of chairperson or team leader, when your mother unexpectedly walks into the room. What is your role now?

In a situation like this, where what is expected of you in one role clashes with what is expected in another role, you can be said to be in **role conflict**.

Another condition occurs where the expectations of your role are different in different people: this is known as **role incompatibility**. For example, your team may prefer you to be the easy-going boss, while your manager expects you to be tough and uncompromising.

Role incompatibility can also occur where your **own** standards don't agree with the organization's standards, or where the image you have of yourself doesn't coincide with other people's. You could imagine a soldier who is told to shoot into a rioting mob being under great stress through role incompatibility.

To reduce the stress caused by role conflict or incompatibility:

- stick to your principles of integrity and don't allow yourself to be compromised;
- try separating your life into compartments: evenings and weekends for your social life, daytime for work life, for example;
- be yourself – people will learn from your behaviour what to expect from you.

It isn't unknown for people to have to take on numerous roles at the same time. A familiar example is the teacher; a typical teacher has the multiple roles of: counsellor, disciplinarian, educator, caretaker, technician, adviser, accountant, child-minder . . . and so on. If you are or have been a teacher, you may care to complete the list yourself! Having too many roles can lead to role overload, which is really an exaggerated form of role conflict. Many team leaders suffer from this condition.

Activity 14

5 mins

You may feel that you have too many roles to play in your job. What can anyone suffering from role overload do about it? Try to suggest **two** things.

_____

_____

_____

_____

If you are already a team leader you are probably already coping with a number of different roles, some of which will conflict. You could:

■ decide priorities, by assigning levels of importance;
■ delegate certain roles to other people;
■ (perhaps) agree with your manager that some functions be removed from your job specification.

5.3 Role underload

The opposite of role overload is role underload. It occurs when an individual feels that he or she is capable of more roles or a bigger role.

Role underload can also be stressful, because it affects self-image. People doing jobs which they feel are below their capabilities will be dissatisfied and probably inefficient.

The organization can unwittingly make things worse by telling employees how capable they are and what great prospects they have, and then proceeding to ask them to play very junior and undemanding roles. This can have the effect of making people feel very dissatisfied.

Activity 15

5 mins

Suppose you take over a new team and you feel that some of the members are probably being underutilized. Owing to the limitations of the job, there isn't a great deal of scope for expanding roles. How might you tackle this situation?

Write down your answer briefly, after a few minutes' thought.

_____

_____

_____

_____

_____

_____

_____

_____

_____

_____

_____

_____

_____

You may have suggested:

■ assigning roles which match capabilities wherever possible;
■ encouraging good work and effort, without building unrealistic hopes or promising opportunities which may not be realized;
■ perhaps talking to your fellow team leaders to see whether reassigning some members to other teams would be possible and beneficial to all concerned.

You may agree that role underload is probably just as common as role overload. These are the kind of problems that are a challenge to the team leader.

Self-assessment 2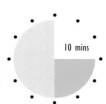

1   What is the team leader's main responsibility?

2   Fill in the blanks in the following sentences then use your answers to complete the grid below. When you have filled in the grid there should be another complete word in the highlighted vertical column. Some of the letters have already been filled in on the grid to give you a clue.

The responsibilities of a team leader towards the _____ in the team are:

■   to _____ and _____ the individual;
■   to _____ tasks appropriate to the member's abilities;
■   to _____ _____ the job roles of the team members;
■   to _____ performance;
■   (if necessary) to _____ the individual from other people, including other members of the group.

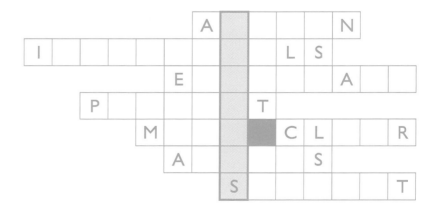

3   Identify the **incorrect** statements among the following, and explain why they are wrong.

a   The team have a right to expect commitment and support from the leader, and to be able to look to the leader to clarify team roles.
b   The leader is a central hub of activity and interest. All communications between management, the team, and other groups, must pass through the leader.
c   Role ambiguity means that there is uncertainty about a person's role at any one time.
d   Role underload means having too little to do.

Answers to these questions can be found on pages 88–9.

6 Summary

- The leader has responsibilities to the task, the team and the individual.

- Achievement of the task is the team leader's main responsibility.

- The responsibility of team leaders towards individuals includes:

  - supporting and encouraging the individual;
  - assigning tasks appropriate to the member's abilities;
  - making clear the job roles of the team members;
  - assessing performance;
  - (if necessary) protecting the individual from other people, including other members of the group.

- So far as the team is concerned, the team leader is responsible for:

  - demonstrating a commitment to the team;
  - setting out and agreeing the overall and specific aims and objectives, so that everyone knows what has to be done and why it has to be done;
  - helping to ensure the standards of the group are maintained;
  - supporting the team when things are going against it.

- The team leader is also normally charged with:

  - representing the team to management;
  - representing management to the team;
  - co-ordinating with other teams and departments.

- Uncertainty about roles is called role ambiguity.

- When what is expected of you in one role clashes with what is expected in another role, you can be said to be in role conflict.

- When the expectations of your role are different in different people, this is known as role incompatibility.

- Role underload occurs when a individual feels that he or she is capable of more roles or a bigger role.

Session C
Leadership styles

1 Introduction

Every team is made up of different individuals. Each individual brings their own skills, attributes, attitudes, strengths and flaws to the team. In a team situation all that these individuals might have in common is membership of the team, with few shared interests or goals.

Leading this team is the primary task of the team leader. An easy way to realize the importance of the leader to the team is to imagine what the team would be like without them. What would happen? Individual team members might carry out particular tasks, but they probably wouldn't have any sense of purpose or clarity. They might not understand why the tasks needed to be carried out in the first place, and results would probably never rise above the mediocre.

A leader must take account of how individuals interact within the group, leading each and every one of them to achieve the common ends of the team. The leader must be adaptable, using all the information and resources available to them.

Achieving good leadership requires the leader to adopt a leadership style that is appropriate to the team at any given time. This enables the leader to support the team in performing effectively. This approach is known as *situational leadership*. Situational leadership considers that there are four key factors affecting team performance:

- the leader;
- the task;
- the team;
- the operational environment.

EXTENSION 4
An account of situational leadership is given in Paul Hersey's book *The Situational Leader.*

In this session we will explore each of these factors in turn, examining how they should be taken into account when working out an appropriate style of leadership.

2 The leader

A team leader needs to know and understand what impact their behaviour has on the team, its individual members and ultimately its performance. Different behaviours relate to different leadership styles.

2.1 Leadership styles

Within your working life you have probably observed different leaders use very different styles of leadership. You may also have noticed a leader adopt more than one style of leadership in response to varying circumstances.

To be effective as a team leader you need to understand what is involved in each style of leadership, and then to develop a sense of where *you* feel most comfortable and what *your team* needs.

We can describe leadership styles as falling into four types.

Authoritative style

The leader:

■ gives instructions and directions;
■ states how the task or tasks are to be done;
■ controls information;
■ establishes and uses channels of communication;
■ allocates roles and responsibilities;
■ supervises all aspects of team activity and interactivity.

Consultative style

The leader:

- gives instructions;
- offers feedback to boost performance and self-esteem;
- closely monitors performance;
- takes occasional notice of team member ideas.

Supportive style

The leader:

- becomes an active team member;
- involves all team members in decision-making;
- re-allocates roles and responsibilities where evidence supports change;
- shares responsibility for decision-making;
- allows team to take decisions;
- exchanges feedback to improve performance.

Delegative style

The leader:

- steps away from the team;
- advises when relevant and appropriate;
- devolves team management to the team itself.

In order to adopt a particular style, or shift between styles, the leader needs a high degree of flexibility, which relies on understanding:

- how and why people behave and react in different situations and circumstances;
- what skills and knowledge are possessed within the team, across all members, including the leader.

It is important to recognize that no one style is always effective, because of the changing nature of various factors.

2.2 The Leadership Style Continuum

Different leadership styles can be observed in a leader's behaviour – different styles tend to produce different types of behaviours. Effective leaders need to be able to recognise these types of behaviour, as, by doing so, they will get an insight into their own and others' leadership style.

These behaviours can be grouped into two main types – *authoritative* and *supportive*. Authoritative behaviours tend to be associated with both the

Authoritative and Consultative leadership styles, Supportive behaviours with both the Supportive and Delegative styles. These two sets of behaviour are described as *overlaying* two leadership styles each, as shown below.

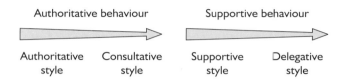

Authoritative behaviour is (as you might expect) most strongly associated with an Authoritative style of leadership. It is also associated, although less strongly, with a Consultative leadership style. Similarly, Supportive behaviours are most strongly associated with a Supportive leadership style, less so with a Delegative style.

Underpinning these two different sets of behaviours are shifts in the leader's focus, from the *tasks* people have to perform, to the *people* themselves. Authoritative leaders, adopting authoritative behaviours, will have the strongest focus on the tasks that need completing. Delegative leaders, at the other extreme, will be most strongly focused on people. The shift in focus, from task to people, is a continuum, as shown in the diagram below.

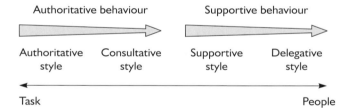

2.3 Leadership behaviours

We have seen that **authoritative behaviour** involves exercising high levels of control and direction and a strong focus on the job in hand.

Activity 16 · 3 mins

Write down two examples where you have observed authoritative behaviour to be used successfully. Why do think they were successful?

_____

_____

One set of situations in which authoritative behaviour can be appropriate is where a rapid response is needed to deal with change. This change could be in the membership of the team, or in the overall objectives or purpose of the team itself. In these situations the leader concerned needs to take control and to show that they are in control.

Supportive behaviour has a very different emphasis. The leader who displays this behaviour is encouraging, supports two-way communication with all concerned and focuses on the people and their involvement. The styles which this behaviour overlays (the supportive and delegative styles) can seem like the most attractive ones. Here the emphasis is more on the people than the task. Although supportive behaviour and its associated styles may seem desirable, they may not be as effective in particular situations – and a team will not thank a leader for adopting them when more authoritative behaviour is required.

Activity 17 · 5 mins

Identify a team situation where you have seen extensive supportive behaviour being demonstrated by the team leader. Was this effective or not? Explain why supportive behaviour might not have been effective.

_____

_____

_____

_____

If the individual members of the team work well together and have reached a stage where they are able to exchange views and arrive, quickly, at decisions, then the leader may find it appropriate to support this process, rather than to direct the team's actions.

However, there are many situations where more authoritative behaviour is required. This may be because the team has not yet reached a stage where they can manage themselves. Or it may be that the nature of their work is time critical and requires an authoritative leader to take control; for example, in a busy restaurant kitchen where the team looks to the chef to tell them what to do and when to do it.

In the next three sections we will examine the other factors that affect the leadership approaches to be adopted.

3 The task

3.1 Overall purpose

'Leadership is sometimes defined as "getting other people to do what you want to do because they want to do it". I do not agree. If it is your task, why should anyone help you to achieve it? It has to be a common task, one which everyone in the group can share because they see that it has value for the organization or society and – directly or indirectly for themselves as well.'

John Adair, *Effective Leadership.*

'The task' is a simple way of defining what the team exists to do: its common purpose. The leader needs to make sure that each and every member of the team shares an understanding as to:

- the actual purpose of the team;
- the objectives of the team.

As well as having this understanding the team needs to believe in the outcome, and see the outcome as achievable. The way the leader establishes this understanding, and the detail in which purpose and objectives are given, will all support this belief.

Shared understanding and belief in the purpose, aims and objectives of the team are essential to the ultimate success of the team.

By describing the team's purpose and its objectives (see 3.2) in clear terms, the leader is more likely to gain the necessary level of understanding. The leader should avoid using too much jargon or complicated terminology, because at certain points team members may have to explain their team to others; if they cannot do this without causing confusion, they will feel less inclined to support the team's overall purpose.

The team's purpose should be explained, and explainable, in clear and simple words – this will support shared understanding and belief.

Activity 18

Describe the purpose of a team that you lead or are a member of.

_____

_____

_____

_____

Would all members of the team be able to describe the purpose in similar terms?

_____

_____

_____

_____

Your answers will be unique to your situation. For example, the purpose of the exhibition team in a local museum may be to mount three major exhibitions every year that pull together different aspects of the museum's collections. In this example, for the team to be effective, all the members should be able to describe this purpose.

If there is no purpose to a team's existence, then it is likely that a true team will never be formed. What then remains is simply a group of individuals who come together occasionally.

3.2 Framing objectives

For a team to achieve its purpose there are several objectives that need to be fulfilled. It is essential that these objectives contribute to the larger aims and objectives of the organization. Consider this flowchart.

The overall function of the team needs to relate to the bigger picture, as presented by the organization. Imagine the series of objectives illustrated above, as a jigsaw puzzle. When all the different objectives across the organization are fitted together they should form a comprehensive picture of that organization. All the objectives from departmental, team and individual level should 'add up' to the organizational objectives. If the team objectives were not clearly related or well-defined there would be jigsaw pieces that did not fit, or extra pieces left over. Any excess pieces would indicate that the team activity may be superfluous to organizational activity.

Activity 19

3 mins

How does your work team contribute to the organization's aims and objectives?

_____

_____

_____

_____

Your answer will be unique to your working situation. In the local museum mentioned earlier, the museum serves the local community, and each exhibition must demonstrate a different aspect of community life, past and present.

As a leader you must understand the ways in which the team's objectives relate to the bigger picture, for example, at departmental level. In order to explain these objectives to the team you must have all the necessary information to hand. If you are not able to satisfy their questions and provide all the detail that they need in order to have a belief in the team, its purpose and objectives, then it will be difficult to get beyond the first stage of that team's development.

The credibility of the leader partly lies in their ability to respond to team member questions and queries, to help them understand their purpose, the overall team objectives.

Ideally, all task-related objectives will be SMART.

S pecific
M easurable
A chievable
R elevant
T ime bound.

Specific

An objective should state clearly what is involved – what needs to be done – using language that makes sense to all involved.

Measurable

All objectives should be defined in a way that enables assessment, or measurement. As you saw in session B, it is important that everyone knows when the objective has been achieved, or indeed when it has been exceeded. If there is no measurement attached to the objective it can be impossible to determine real success.

Many argue that it is impossible to make all objectives ones that can be easily measured. For example, quantities are more easily measured than qualities. If the team is required to improve the level of tidiness in an office, for example, then the leader must agree with the team what 'tidiness' will 'look like'. What will no longer be on desks at the end of the day? When will rubbish be cleared?

It can be useful to use visual terms in an objective, where changes and differences can be easily seen by all involved.

Example

Davies Ltd is a small, but growing, company providing technical writing services to computer software companies. Davies need to relocate to larger premises while minimizing disruption to their normal work. The managing director, Rachel Middleton, sets up a small team of five key individuals to manage the process of the move. One suitable objective for this team is:

on completion of the project on 30 August 2003, each individual will have a working area of 6m square.

Achievable

Whatever the objectives, they must be achievable. If objectives are unattainable team members will quickly realize this, and levels of support can decline. As teams begin to gather evidence of their successes, they will often strive to achieve something extra, and exceed the original objectives and targets.

A pre-requisite to making objectives achievable is for you to ensure that your team has the *resources* it needs. Where possible, agree the objectives with your team and consult them on the resources required. Agreeing targets increases the incentive to reach them. Imposing work objectives without consultation, or without providing the opportunity for team members to explore what is involved, may result in resentment.

As the team develops the team leader may feel that the time is right to let the team set their own objectives. This may work well where the team is working on a long-term basis, where their operational role changes over time.

Relevant

There are two ways in which your objectives should be *relevant*.

First, objectives must be relevant to the team: that is, they must be such that the team can have a direct affect on them.

Secondly, objectives must be relevant to your organization. They must fit with your organization's wider objectives. Resist the temptation to set easily achievable objectives that are not strictly relevant to your organization's prime goals. Objectives should focus your team's attention on key areas.

Time bound

Some targets are easily time bound. Production targets, for example, can be set on a daily, weekly or monthly basis. Other objectives need to be time constrained too so that a sense of accomplishment is possible at predefined points in the team's operational activity.

Where objectives are not easily set in time bound terms, agree review periods, where review of performance to date can determine how far the objectives have been achieved.

3.3 Building a vision

The leader is responsible for providing the team with a realistic vision for its overall purpose and achievement of objectives. Ongoing communication of this vision will serve to build a cohesive and enthusiastic team. Continuous two-way dialogue, using the SMART objectives as its basis, will give the team a better sense of the shared nature of its purpose.

In section 4 we will consider how to review and amend objectives in terms of leadership style.

4 The team

'People are not the same. They are as different as thumbprints. People are different up and down, through and through, coming and going – in their likes, dislikes, fears, joys, the way they think and decide, the way they work and communicate. Teams succeed when they acknowledge this fact of natural variation, and work to recognize and value differences among their members.'

Harvey Robbins and Michael Finley, *Why Teams Don't Work*, Texere 2000

EXTENSION 2
An account of the stages of team development is given in the book *Teambuilding* by Alastair Fraser and Suzanne Neville.

As individuals enter and move through team working processes they go through four distinct stages of team development.

■ Forming
■ Storming
■ Norming
■ Performing

We will examine each of these stages and consider which leadership style may be most appropriate during each.

This cycle of team development is a useful way of examining how best to lead a team, at different points.

4.1 Forming

Team formation is a time of uncertainty, where members are trying to establish what is to happen, what their part is likely to be and how they will work with the others. They will look to the leader to offer clarity of purpose, guidance on what the accepted standards of behaviour are to be, and a clear steer on the roles and responsibilities of each individual.

Forming is the stage where change is to the fore. As a leader you may be able to select or contribute to the selection of team members. If you are able to be involved in selection, ask the following questions.

- What is the purpose of the team?
- What are the essential skills and knowledge required to fulfil this purpose?
- Where do these skills and knowledge lie at present?
- How might the potential mix of individuals work together?
- How will I ensure that these individuals can become a team?

Activity 20 · 5 mins

During the **forming** stage of a team's development, what leadership style do you believe is likely to be most effective, and why?

_____

_____

_____

An authoritative style may well be most effective during this stage, as the leader will need to set ground rules, clarify objectives and allocate roles and responsibilities.

Another important aspect of this stage is to help the team establish an identity. This can be in the form of a name or title, which may include a statement of the team's purpose.

Example

In the example of Davies Ltd, a suitable title for the team is: the Relocation Team, indicating that the team's purpose is the relocation of the office.

One very important point about the forming stage is that it can re-occur at several times during the team's life cycle. Where a new team member is introduced, or established members leave, change is inevitable. Indeed the forming stage is primarily about change. Another point to remember is that this stage will occur when a new leader is introduced.

Forming is the stage of team development that is mostly concerned with change and uncertainty.

4.2 Storming

During the **storming** stage team members are entering a discovery phase, where conflict can occur.

Activity 21

5 mins)

What are team members trying to discover during this stage? List up to four things.

_____

_____

_____

_____

Individuals are probably trying to discover a number of things, including: their real place on the team; their relationships with others; expected standards of behaviour; the extent and complexity of the task; the resources available to support achievement of the task; their relationship with the leader.

Conflict results from a degree of uncertainty; it is the responsibility of the leader to adopt a style and approach that will enable conflict to be successfully resolved.

Conflict can result where individuals embark upon a route of discovery during the storming stage of team development.

Activity 22 · 3 mins

What leadership style/s would be most appropriate in resolving conflict and enabling individuals to discover their place on the team?

_____

_____

_____

_____

A combination of authoritative and consultative styles is most likely to be effective here. The need for encouraging self-esteem in individual members will support their integration. An establishment of workable communication channels will also ensure a transition to the next stage in the development cycle.

4.3 Norming

A **norm** can be defined as a standard of behaviour that is derived from what the members of the group perceive as being acceptable and appropriate.

At this stage the team starts to recognize evidence of their successes, as well illustrations of their failures. Evidence of teamworking will also be seen by others outside the team, and the team will be perceived as an entity in its own right. The team exists.

The group begins to demonstrate a team identity, which is acknowledged by others. Team confidence also becomes obvious, and is supported by the evidence.

Activity 23

5 mins

How might team confidence show itself?

_____

_____

_____

_____

_____

_____

_____

_____

Evidence of team confidence might show itself as: willingness to listen to the opinions of others; a pride in the team; a pride in being a member of the team; genuine cohesiveness and a readiness to share; mutual support and shared responsibility; a readiness to take action.

One difficulty that can arise during the norming stage is that the team can become so sure of itself that it wants to work in isolation, setting itself up as a body of experts. The very norms that the team establishes, of behaviour and action, may be at odds with the norms of the department or organization as a whole. The team leader needs to be aware of the signs, and take action to discourage this isolationist approach.

Sound and practical plans will be needed to support the team in meeting its objectives. These plans must:

- be consistent with the SMART objectives;
- provide for all individuals within the team, taking account of their abilities and development needs of each;
- be realistic and achievable within the constraints imposed on and by the organization;
- be conveyed to the team in sufficient detail, and at a level and pace that individuals can cope with;
- be updated at regular intervals, because plans have to meet changing needs, and unforeseen circumstances.

Activity 24 ·

3 mins

Consider the essential requirements of team planning. What leadership style would support successful team planning, during the norming stage of team development?

_____

_____

Because planning is focused on supporting individuals, helping them to feel empowered to work well within the team, a participative style with supportive behaviour is likely to be most effective here.

4.4 Performing

This is the time in a team's development when it begins to produce useful work. Conflict will have subsided, and members settled into their roles.

Activity 25 ·

5 mins

What are the potential pitfalls for the team leader during this stage of the team's development?

_____

_____

_____

What style of leadership would help to enable them to deal with these pitfalls?

_____

A delegative style may well work here, with the leader devolving leadership. The pitfalls that might be encountered may include:

■ a need to be seen to be leading – shifting back to the left hand of the continuum and placing oneself in a role of authority, removing this from the other team members;

- sitting back and letting the team work, without providing support and guidance when required;
- complacency, particularly where the team has begun to perform well.

The leader should be:

- monitoring the output and quality of the work, to ensure that it meets the agreed targets;
- ensuring performance is maintained;
- supporting the team in seeking new challenges and targets, aiming to improve performance, where possible.

At this stage, as with the others, the leader must lead by example, while drawing the best from the team and its individual members. Feedback between team members will support this phase. Team members, including the leader, need to be aware of where their contributions have made significant difference to achievement of objectives.

Feedback will support development of the individuals and the team as a whole.

4.5 Mourning

Another stage a team may have to experience is that of mourning. Mourning arises when a team is disbanded. For example, if a team is working on a short-term project basis it will be disbanded when it has achieved its purpose.

Activity 26 · 5 mins

What do you believe is the role of the team leader during the mourning stage?

_____

_____

_____

What leadership style would be most effective at this stage?

_____

Individual members of the team may not wish to focus on the point of closure, so it will be helpful if the team leader can take responsibility for organizing this stage. The leader needs to take responsibility for the winding-down process, so they may need to shift back through the continuum to a consultative style. Individual team members are likely to feel quite sad, particularly if the team has worked well together.

If possible, the team leader should plan in advance for this point of closure and prepare their team members. They should provide feedback to each individual in the team, to help them to review their work in the team and prepare for the next phase of their working life. The team leader should also organize an event to celebrate the achievement of the team and mark a point of closure for its activities.

Providing feedback

Mourning can be seen as a continuation of the performing stage: it is important for each member of the team to understand where their strengths lie as a result of their teamworking. The leader should offer feedback that addresses:

- the areas of team performance where the individual made significant contributions;
- where the individual's skills can make a real contribution in any future team work, or in their day-to-day job role;
- areas of performance that would benefit from development, with suggestions as to which forms the development might take.

If possible, the leader should facilitate feedback from team colleagues to each individual, as a way of boosting confidence. Individuals often value feedback from peers if it is offered constructively, with suggestions for improvement. To make sure that the feedback is constructive and focuses on positive performance, the leader should take an active facilitative role.

Constructive feedback can be developmental and help individuals to transfer skills into other areas of their work.

Planning for the mourning stage

If the team is working to limited timescales then the leader should make plans at an early stage that include the following.

- A specific date for when the team activity will official close. This date can be incorporated into the SMART objectives, which will help the team members get used to the idea.
- How feedback will be offered, on what basis, and what the purpose of this feedback will be for the team as a whole, and for each individual.
- A social get-together for all team members, which will serve as a farewell event for everyone.

5 The operational environment

So far we have looked at the *leader*, the *task* and the *team*. The fourth factor that affects team leadership is the **environment** in which the team must operate.

An operational environment includes:

- the organization itself;
- the actual working environment;
- the external environment.

5.1 The organization

Every organization has its own structure and culture. Each individual is expected to uphold certain values in their approaches to work. Across the organization leaders and managers may develop ways of working that require them to adopt particular leadership styles. In many cases styles of leadership and management reflect the culture and values of the organization.

Where an organization has a hierarchical structure, with many different levels of management and supervision, an authoritative style may predominate. An organization with a 'flatter' structure, where managers are used to delegating responsibility, may result in the predominance of a participative or delegative style of leadership.

Activity 27   5 mins

How would you describe the structure of your organization? What style of leadership do you believe results from the structure?

_____

_____

_____

It is helpful to recognize the impact that your own organizational structure can have on leadership style. If team members are used to a particular style of leadership, either in their day-to-day work, or as a result of other teamworking experiences, then you as leader need to take this into account when determining the most appropriate style of leadership for your team.

5.2 Actual working environment

Every team has to work within existing environments. When a work team is set up to address a special project within its own department, suddenly individuals have to establish different relationships with each other, both within and outside the team. Team members may come from a range of different departments, and individuals may be used to better, or in some cases, worse facilities or resources.

Activity 28 · 3 mins

What working environment factors might have an adverse effect on members of your team? List up to three and identify approaches for addressing these.

_____

_____

_____

Working environment issues must be considered, particularly at the storming stage. Conflicts may be the result of external factors that are outside the team leader's control, but it is essential that, as leader, you are aware of the impact of the working environment on team cohesion.

5.3 The external environment

The external environment can and does have a considerable impact on all aspects of the organization and its activities. Factors such as competition, legislation and changes to regulations and supplier and customer activity all have some effect on day-to-day performance, and a potential effect on team activity.

Activity 29

5 mins

Identify up to three external environment issues that could have an impact on the purpose and objectives of your team. How would you communicate these, and what information would be essential to team understanding?

_____

_____

_____

_____

As the team leader you need to keep informed of any changes that are the result of external environment. It is not likely that you can do much about, for example, legislative changes, but you can communicate how they will affect the team. Communicating information of this nature needs to be done at the right level and pace, being sure not to bombard team members with information that has little if any bearing on the team and its objectives.

6 Personal leadership style

So far in this session, we have considered leadership styles with respect to the needs of the task, the team and the operational environment. In this section we will look at the issue from the perspective of _your individual personality and skills_. We will examine your current preferences in terms of leadership style, and identify any skills development needs that might be appropriate.

6.1 Style preferences

Activity 30 · 10 mins

Reflect on the leadership style descriptions in section 2.1. Which is the style that you adopt most frequently in your leadership roles? Why do you believe this is the case?

_____

_____

_____

_____

Consider a recent leadership role that you have held. What effect did the leadership style that you adopted have on the team? Give two examples of positive and two examples of negative impact, if possible.

_____

_____

_____

_____

_____

The important point here is that there is no right or wrong style. Any leader must take account of the various factors relating to the task, the team and the operational environment, while at the same time recognizing where their own preferences lie.

To adopt different and appropriate styles a leader requires flexibility and a sound understanding of how the different factors impact on team performance.

6.2 Styles and skills

Each leadership style is associated both with particular behaviours, as we have seen in section 2.2, and with particular skills.

Activity 31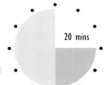

20 mins

For each leadership style we have listed below associated skills. To get a clear picture of your development needs complete each table in detail. If possible you may wish to get input from a colleague, or colleagues, in order to get a clearer picture of your leadership development needs.

Authoritative style

Skills required	Do I possess it?	Colleague assessment
Creating and sharing a vision	Yes/no	Yes/no
Setting SMART objectives	Yes/no	Yes/no
Allocating tasks	Yes/no	Yes/no
Allocating roles and responsibilities	Yes/no	Yes/no
Monitoring performance	Yes/no	Yes/no
Controlling activities	Yes/no	Yes/no
Observation of individual performance	Yes/no	Yes/no
Observation of team performance	Yes/no	Yes/no
Giving constructive feedback	Yes/no	Yes/no
Ideas for development of skills, where need identified		

Consultative style

Skills required	Do I possess it?	Colleague assessment
Provide constructive support	Yes/no	Yes/no
Facilitating discussion	Yes/no	Yes/no
Handling conflict	Yes/no	Yes/no
Resolving conflict	Yes/no	Yes/no
Listening	Yes/no	Yes/no
Reviewing with others	Yes/no	Yes/no
Ideas for development of skills, where need identified		

Supportive style

Skills required	Do I possess it?	Colleague assessment
Facilitating development	Yes/no	Yes/no
Providing support and practical information	Yes/no	Yes/no
Challenging inappropriate behaviour	Yes/no	Yes/no
Listening	Yes/no	Yes/no
Motivating	Yes/no	Yes/no
Realigning SMART objectives	Yes/no	Yes/no
Ideas for development of skills, where need identified		

Delegative style

Skills required	Do I possess it?	Colleague assessment
Delegating responsibilities	Yes/no	Yes/no
Delegating tasks	Yes/no	Yes/no
Motivating for growth	Yes/no	Yes/no
Disbanding teams	Yes/no	Yes/no
Giving constructive feedback	Yes/no	Yes/no
Facilitating feedback between colleagues	Yes/no	Yes/no
Ideas for development of skills, where need identified		

6.3 Planning leadership styles development

In the previous activity you have begun to list ideas for development of the skills that support the different styles across the continuum. If you were unable to get comments from a colleague on your skills needs, then discuss your development ideas with someone who can help you to build a clear picture of your needs.

Self-knowledge and self-awareness are both qualities required by any leader. In order to develop these qualities a leader needs to seek and act upon feedback. This feedback should be sought from a range of sources, including team members, other colleagues and their line manager. At the same time a leader needs to be observant, taking account of the impact of their behaviour on others.

Self-assessment 3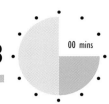

00 mins

Complete the following sentences with a suitable word or words, chosen from the list below.

1 The four key factors affecting team performance are: _____,
_____, _____ and _____.

2 Authoritative behaviour overlays the _____ style and
_____ style of leadership.

3 Team formation is a time of _____, where members are trying
to establish what is to happen, what their part is likely to be and how they will
work with the others.

4 _____ can be developmental and help individuals
to transfer skills into other areas of their work.

5 Conflict can result where individuals embark upon a route of discovery during
the _____ stage of team development.

6 A leader needs to be _____, taking account of the
impact of their behaviour on others.

THE TASK	STORMING	THE TEAM
THE MANAGER	CONSULTATIVE	CONSTRUCTIVE FEEDBACK
UNCERTAINTY	THE LEADER	THE OPERATIONAL ENVIRONMENT
OPEN	AUTHORITATIVE	TRANSPARENT
NORMING	OBSERVANT	

7 Identify which of the following statements are correct and explain why you
disagree with the others.

a There is no right or wrong style, a leader needs to adopt a flexible
approach to the team and its situation.
b A leader needs to keep to the style that is the most effective for them.
c In resolving conflict a leader must smooth things over so that the problem
is easily forgotten by everyone.

8 Select the one incorrect statement from the list below, and explain why it is wrong.

In dealing with the norming stage the leader should:

a focus on supporting individuals, and apply a participative style, with supportive behaviour;
b adopt authoritative behaviour because the team can easily begin to move away from organizational norms as they develop their own;
c build sound and practical plans to support the team in meeting its objectives.

Answers to these questions can be found on page 89.

7 Summary

- The four factors that affect a team's performance are:
  - the leader;
  - the task;
  - the team;
  - the operational environment.

- Different behaviours, authoritative and supportive, overlay a continuum of styles.

- The continuum of styles runs left to right, from authoritative to consultative to participative to delegative. The shift of emphasis runs from task to people as the continuum shifts from left to right.

- Authoritative behaviour overlays authoritative and consultative leadership styles.

- Supportive behaviour overlays participative and delegative leader styles.

- A team can only function effectively if it understands what its purpose is, and how this fits into the organization and its objectives overall.

- Ideally all task-related objectives will be SMART:

  S pecific
  M easurable
  A chievable
  R elevant
  T ime bound

- The four main stages of team development are: forming, storming, norming and performing. Another potential stage is mourning, where a team disbands after a period of time.

- Different leadership styles are appropriate for each of the different stages of team development.

- Constructive feedback can be developmental and help individuals to transfer skills into other areas of their work.

- Self-knowledge and self-awareness are both qualities required by any leader.

Performance checks

1 Quick quiz

Jot down the answers to the following questions on *Leading Your Team*.

Question 1   'In work organizations, managers are team leaders, and team leaders are managers.' Say to what extent you agree with this statement, and briefly explain why.

_____

_____

_____

_____

Question 2   List **three** 'personal qualities' that are looked for in a team leader.

_____

_____

_____

Question 3   We listed the steps of decision-making as: 1 Defining the problem; 2 Collecting information; 3 Generating alternatives; 4 Choosing the best option; 5 Implementing your choice; 6 Evaluating the result. Typically, which steps do inconsistent decision-makers tend to spend too little time on?

_____

_____

_____

Question 4 'The best leaders never ask their team members to do something they couldn't do themselves.' Is this statement true, do you think? Briefly explain your answer.

_____

_____

_____

Question 5 Our three-circle model listed the three main responsibilities of the leader. What are they?

_____

_____

_____

Question 6 List **three** responsibilities that the team leader has towards the individual.

_____

_____

_____

Question 7 Now list **three** responsibilities that the team leader has towards the team as a group.

_____

_____

_____

Question 8 What kinds of prompting questions would help the team to assess its own performance?

_____

_____

_____

Question 9   Explain what you think is meant by: 'the leader represents management to the team'.

_____

_____

_____

Question 10   Match each term on the left with the correct description on the right.

a Role ambiguity.	w A clash between what is expected of you in one role and what is expected in another role.
b Role underload.	x When different people have different expectations about someone's role.
c Role incompatibility.	y Uncertainty about roles.
d Role conflict.	z When an individual feels that he or she is capable of more roles or a bigger role.

Question 11   What are the **four** factors that affect team performance?

_____

_____

_____

_____

Question 12   What types of behaviour overlay the four styles of leadership? Which behaviours relate particularly to the different leadership styles?

_____

_____

_____

_____

Question 13   What does the term SMART mean in relation to setting objectives? Explain what each letter stands for.

_____

_____

_____

_____

Question 14   Why might conflict arise during storming stage of team development?

_____

_____

_____

_____

Question 15   Name up to four of the skills that are required within the consultative style of leadership.

_____

_____

_____

_____

Answers to these questions can be found on pages 91–3.

60 mins

2 Workbook assessment

Marti came to work at a small training company after working as a supervisor in the finance department of a public-sector organization for 10 years. The training company had been set up by two individuals who had each worked independently as customer service trainers for several years. The company had 25 employees, and Marti was appointed leader of a project team made up of two administrators and three trainers. The team was expected to investigate potential training business opportunities within a particular segment of manufacturing, across the UK. Marti was appointed because of her sound financial background and supervisory experience, but it was acknowledged that her understanding of training was limited.

Answer the following questions. You do not need to write more than three or four sentences for each answer.

1 Which leadership qualities would Marti need to emphasize, given her limited expertise in the field of training? How could she demonstrate these qualities to her team?

2 What should Marti consider when she represents her team to management? What forms of performance assessment would support this representation?

3 Given Marti's background, what type of leadership style(s) might she want to bring to the team? How appropriate would this be in the circumstances? If not appropriate, what leadership style(s) could Marti seek to adopt, and why?

4 Define the purpose of the team as clearly and briefly as you can. From the limited information available, produce up to two SMART objectives that would be appropriate for this team.

5 Having identified appropriate leadership style(s), which skills should Marti focus on, and which do you believe she may already possess? Give your reasons for the choices you make.

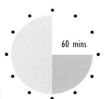

60 mins

3 Work-based assignment

S/NVQ C1.1

The time guide for this assignment gives you an approximate idea of how long it is likely to take you to write up your findings. You will find you need to spend some additional time gathering information, perhaps talking to colleagues and thinking about the assignment.

Your written response to this assignment may provide the basis of appropriate evidence for your S/NVQ portfolio.

What you have to do

For this assignment, your aim is to find ways of improving the effectiveness of yourself as a team leader.

1 You will need to conduct an analysis of your performance. It is very difficult to do this without help, so you will need to consult others, such as your manager, members of your team, and perhaps other friendly colleagues. Tell them you are looking for honest and constructive criticism, in assessing your skills and performance. Only ask those whom you feel would give helpful answers.

> Activity 3 on page 19 is relevant to this assignment.

The following list of questions is fairly comprehensive. One approach is to set them out on sheets of paper, and ask each person to give you a mark out of 10. (You may prefer them to do this anonymously, so they won't be inhibited through fear of hurting your feelings.) You can then add up the scores for each item, and average the scores. Thus you might get scores of 8, 7, 5 and 10 for 'planning', giving a total of 30 and an average of 7.5.

2 Once you have collected and analysed your responses, you are in a good position to identify your strengths and weaknesses, and to improve your performance. In order to eliminate your weak spots, you could, for example:

■ request specific training;
■ find a mentor to help you;
■ simply decide to change your attitude and approach.

One thing you may want to give some thought to is whether you should be acting less as a traditional-style manager, giving instructions and controlling the work, and more as a facilitator, empowering the team to make its own decisions.

You will need to consider the following questions.

- How good are my management skills, i.e.,
  - planning
  - organizing and co-ordinating
  - monitoring and controlling
  - communicating
  - supporting and motivating
  - evaluating?
- How good am I at showing:
  - determination
  - consistency
  - dependability
  - integrity
  - fairness
  - confidence in the team?
- How good am I at:
  - giving credit where it's due
  - standing by the team when it's in trouble
  - keeping the team informed
  - supporting and encouraging the individual
  - assigning tasks appropriate to the members' abilities
  - making clear the job roles of the team members
  - assessing performance
  - protecting the individual from other people
  - demonstrating a commitment to the team
  - making clear the roles of the team members, so that everyone knows what is expected of them
  - setting out and agreeing the overall and specific aims and objectives, so that everyone knows what has to be done and why
  - helping to ensure that the standards of the group are maintained
  - supporting the team when things are going against it
  - representing the team to management
  - representing management to the team
  - co-ordinating with other teams and departments.

What you should write

You should submit:

- the results of your 'survey';
- a brief commentary on it, e.g. what surprised you about it? What do you disagree with?
- an explanation of the actions you intend to take as a result of the above, for improving your performance.

You should not need to write more than two or three pages in total. The most important purpose of your report is to convince the reader that you have a well-thought out plan for improvement.

Reflect and review

1 Reflect and review

Now that you have completed your work on *Leading Your Team*, let us review our workbook objectives.

> When you have completed this workbook you will be better able to assess your own leadership qualities and potential.

Throughout this workbook, we have attempted to answer questions such as: 'What is a leader?'; 'What does a leader have to be?'; 'What does a leader have to do?' As we have discussed, physical attributes – physical strength, sex, age, etc. – do not seem to be very relevant. As was mentioned in session A, a leader has to have followers and, to get people to follow you, it's necessary to persuade and influence them: to guide their actions and opinions. This can be done in very many ways, and it is important that each would-be leader should behave in a natural manner, rather than try to copy someone else's style.

Now that you have completed your reading, and responded to the activities, you will perhaps have a better understanding of what leadership is, and is not. If so, you should be in a better position to evaluate your own leadership qualities and potential.

Try the following questions.

■ Do you have the determination and confidence to be an excellent leader? Explain your answer, briefly.

_____

_____

_____

_____

_____

■ How would you describe your potential as a leader?

_____

_____

_____

_____

_____

The second objective was as follows.

> When you have completed this workbook you will be better able to enhance your leadership skills.

After assessment come the plans for improvement. As we discussed, most leadership skills and attributes can be learned or acquired, with the possible exception of the most basic ones of determination, a willingness to be a leader, and an enjoyment of working with people. One conclusion that was not quite expressed in so many words in the workbook was that 'almost anyone can be a leader'. Nevertheless, this is probably true. We also noted that leadership was not management, i.e. the functions of leadership and management are not the same. However, there is a good deal of overlap between them.

Like many callings, improvement at leadership comes with practice, **provided that** you have a good understanding of what you're aiming at, and some knowledge of the necessary techniques. One excellent approach is to find a role model – someone whose leadership skills and qualities you admire. If that role model can also act as a trusted advisor, so much the better.

■ Which elements of the techniques or advice discussed are particularly relevant and useful to you, in your aspirations to become a more effective leader?

_____

_____

_____

_____

■ What have you learned that will help you better understand your aims as a leader?

_____

_____

_____

_____

The third objective of the workbook was as follows.

> When you have completed this workbook you will be better able to recognize the responsibilities of leadership, and the roles to be played by a team leader.

For convenience, we used John Adair's three-circle model to identify the triple sets of responsibility: the task, the individual and the team. The task always takes priority, because it is the whole purpose of the team. Among the responsibilities towards the individual team member, we noted: supporting and encouraging the individual; assigning tasks appropriate to the member's abilities; making clear the job roles of the team members; assessing performance; (if necessary) protecting the individual from other people, including other members of the group.

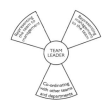

Included in the leader's responsibilities towards the team as a group were: demonstrating a commitment to the team; setting out and agreeing the overall and specific aims and objectives; helping to ensure the standards of the group are maintained; and supporting the team when things are going against it.

The team leader also: represents the team to management; represents management to the team; and co-ordinates with other teams and departments.

The leader may have many roles, which can result in role ambiguity or role conflict; to some extent, this is only to be expected.

■ If you think you have now identified most of the responsibilities you have towards your task, your team and the individuals in it, which of these responsibilities did you previously not recognize?

_____

_____

_____

_____

_____

■ Which roles do you play as team leader?

_____

_____

_____

_____

The last workbook objective was as follows.

When you have completed this workbook you will be better able to identify and adopt a style of leadership appropriate to the needs of the team and its particular situation.

We have considered how there are four factors that affect team performance: the leader, the task, the team and the operational environment.

The **leader** can adopt either authoritative or supportive behaviours. These behaviours overlay a continuum of leadership styles, which include authoritative, consultative, supportive and delegative styles. No one style is more effective than another, but the leader needs to know and understand the other factors that will have an impact. At the same time, a high degree of self-knowledge and self-awareness are needed for the leader to become flexible and able to adopt the leadership styles that suit the situation.

The **task** is a simple way of describing the purpose of the team, in other words the reason that the team exists – what there is to do. Everyone in the team needs to understand the team's purpose, or it will be difficult to achieve. Sound objectives are needed to make sure the purpose is achieved. These objectives should be SMART:

S pecific
M easurable
A chievable
R elevant
T ime bound

Where objectives meet the SMART criteria, shared understanding by all team members is more likely.

The **team** is made up of very different individuals; the leader needs to consider what each individual brings to the team. As the team progresses it will go through a series of development stages: forming, storming, norming and performing. During each stage the leader needs to take account of what is happening, and to adapt their style accordingly. For example, during the forming stage the leader should focus on establishing what is required, by setting SMART objectives. This is likely to be best supported by the adoption of an authoritative style of leadership, where the focus is on the job in hand: the task. As the team progresses through the stages of development a move across the leadership style continuum is likely to apply. A final stage of mourning is also a possibility, where the team disbands after a period of time. During the mourning stage the team members will miss the way they have worked and the successes that they have enjoyed.

Every team is affected, to a greater or lesser degree, by the **environment** in which it works. The operational environment is broken into: the organization (its structure and culture which affect everyone within the business), the actual working environment in which the team has to function and the external environment (which may not have a direct effect on the team, but which requires the leader to take account of how issues from the external environment might affect the team's overall activity).

Finally, we explored where individual preferences might lie and which leadership style is the one with which you feel most at ease. Different skills are needed by a leader when they adopt each of the leadership styles, from authoritative to delegative. A detailed consideration of these skills was offered, with the opportunity to seek feedback from a colleague to help in gauging your effectiveness across each style area.

Here are some final questions to examine.

■ What stage do you believe your team has reached?

_____

_____

_____

■ Is this the right stage given the current situation?

_____

_____

_____

■ If it isn't what might have gone wrong?

_____

_____

_____

■ How has your previous style(s) of leadership affected the stage that the team has reached?

_____

_____

_____

2 Action plan

Use this plan to further develop for yourself a course of action you want to take. Make a note in the left-hand column of the issues or problems you want to tackle, and then decide what you intend to do, and make a note in column 2.

The resources you need might include time, materials, information or money. You may need to negotiate for some of them, but they could be something easily acquired, like half an hour of somebody's time, or a chapter of a book. Put whatever you need in column 3. No plan means anything without a timescale, so put a realistic target completion date in column 4.

Finally, describe the outcome you want to achieve as a result of this plan, whether it is for your own benefit or advancement, or a more efficient way of doing things.

Desired outcomes			
1 Issues	2 Action	3 Resources	4 Target completion
Actual outcomes			

3 Extensions

Extension 1

Book   *Effective Leadership*
Author   John Adair
Edition   1988
Publisher   Pan

This book covers all aspects of leadership. It is stimulating and lively, and is not difficult to read. There are three parts: Understanding Leadership; Developing your Leadership Abilities; Growing as a Leader.

Extension 2

Book   *Teambuilding*
Authors   Alastair Fraser and Suzanne Neville
Edition   1995
Publisher   Spiro Press

A light and easy read, this book covers the main topics of teambuilding. To quote from its introduction: 'This publication is not designed to be a "quick fix" and it certainly won't change your life in 10 minutes, but our purpose is to identify and understand the issues and actions of successful teambuilding.'

Extension 3

Book   *Organizational Behaviour*
Authors   Andrzej Huczynski and David Buchanan
Edition   Fourth edition 2000
Publisher   F T Prentice Hall

This book is written from two points of view: management and the social sciences. It is divided into five parts: the individual in the organization; groups in the organization; technology in the organization; structural influences on behaviour; management in the organization. The most relevant chapters to our subject are: Chapter 15 – Organizational structure and Chapter 19 – Leadership and management style.

Extension 4

Book/audio
   cassette   *The Situational Leader*
Author   Dr Paul Hersey
Publisher   Centre for Leadership Studies/Management
                Learning Resources Ltd

Only available from http://www.situational.com/leadership/accessories.html

Brief and written with clarity, this book/tape explains the Situational Leadership Model through a realistic conversation between two managers.

These extensions can be taken up via your ILM Centre. They will either have them or will arrange that you have access to them. However, it may be more convenient to check out the materials with your human resources people at work – they may well give you access. There are other good reasons for approaching your own people; for example, they will become aware of your interest and you can involve them in your development.

4 Answers to self-assessment questions

Self-assessment 1 on page 21

1   To be a leader, you need DETERMINATION to succeed, and to like working with PEOPLE.

2   People tend to be DEPENDABLE when others EXPECT them to be.

3   To get the RESPECT of a team, you need to be honest with them, and show you care about certain IDEALS.

4   Few of us are always FAIR. All that others can expect of you is that you try very hard to be fair.

5   To be CONSISTENT in your decision-making, be clear in your mind about the problem, and then collect FACTS and OPINIONS before you decide.

6   To LEAD others, it helps to be EXPERIENCED in the work they do.

7   The way that a leader's BEHAVIOUR is viewed by others will largely determine how SUCCESSFUL the leader is.

8   The complete diagram is as follows.

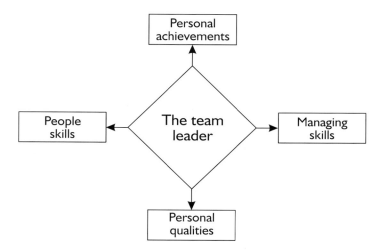

9   The six characteristics recognized as being important in good leadership are:

dependability
ability to listen
good communication skills
integrity
ability to inspire confidence
good managing skills.

Self-assessment 2 on page 40

1   The team leader's main responsibility is to the task.

2   The responsibilities of a team leader towards INDIVIDUALS in the team are:

■ to SUPPORT and ENCOURAGE the individual;
■ to ASSIGN tasks appropriate to the member's abilities;
■ to MAKE CLEAR the job roles of the team members;
■ to ASSESS performance;
■ (if necessary) to PROTECT the individual from other people, including other members of the group.

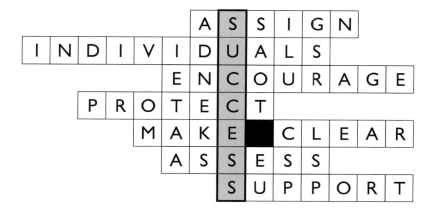

3 There are two **incorrect** statements.

  b The leader is a central hub of activity and interest. All communications between management, the team, and other groups must pass through the leader. (This is not correct, because the team leader does not usually handle all communications 'in and out' of the team, even though he or she is often at the hub of communications.)

  d Role underload means having too little to do. (Role underload means having too few roles, which is not the same thing.)

Self-assessment 3 on pages 68–9

1 The four key factors affecting team performance are: THE LEADER, THE TASK, THE TEAM and THE OPERATIONAL ENVIRONMENT.

2 Authoritative behaviour overlays the AUTHORITATIVE style and CONSULTATIVE style of leadership.

3 Team formation is a time of UNCERTAINTY, where members are trying to establish what is to happen, what their part is likely to be and how they will work with the others.

4 CONSTRUCTIVE FEEDBACK can be developmental and help individuals to transfer skills into other areas of their work.

5 Conflict can result where individuals embark upon a route of discovery during the STORMING stage of team development.

6 A leader needs to be OBSERVANT, taking account of the impact of their behaviour on others.

7 Identify which of the following statements are correct and explain why you disagree with the others.

   Statement a is correct: there is no right or wrong style, a leader needs to adopt a flexible approach to the team and its situation.

   Statements b and c are incorrect because they encourage the leader to focus on their own needs (rather than those of the team, the task and the environment) and to keep things under wraps.

8 Select the one incorrect statement from the list below, and explain why it is wrong:

   Statement b is incorrect because by this stage the team is reaching the point where the focus should be moving towards the people and away from the task.

5 Answers to Activities

**Activity 4
on page 10**

Check your answers against the following.

Categorize the leadership qualities we have listed into the four groups, and then say which of them you think can be learned or acquired.

	People skills	Personal qualities	Managing skills	Personal achievements	Can be learned
The ability to inspire confidence	✓	✓	☐	☐	✓
Determination	☐	✓	☐	☐	?
Dependability	☐	✓	☐	☐	✓
Integrity	☐	✓	☐	☐	✓
A history of success and achievement	☐	☐	☐	✓	✓
Fairness	☐	✓	☐	☐	✓
Listening skills	✓	☐	✓	☐	✓
Consistency	☐	✓	☐	☐	✓
A genuine interest in others	☐	✓	☐	☐	?
Displaying confidence in the team	✓	☐	☐	☐	✓
Giving credit where it's due	✓	☐	☐	☐	✓
The willingness to stand by the team	✓	☐	☐	☐	✓
Being good at keeping the team informed	✓	☐	✓	☐	✓

There are three qualities that are ticked in more than one of the first four columns.

■ **The ability to inspire confidence.**

You might argue that this is a personal quality, because it stems from the behaviour and image of the leader; you could also claim that it is a people skill, as confidence can be gained through talking with them.

■ **Listening skills.**

This is both a people skill and a managing skill, because it is about communication.

■ **Being good at keeping the team informed.**

Another communication skill – the same reasoning applies.

6 Answers to the quick quiz

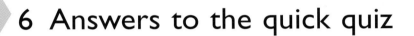

Answer 1   Managers are generally expected to lead teams, but the functions of management do not entirely coincide with the qualities required of leadership.

Answer 2   You could have mentioned: integrity, fairness, consistency or determination.

Answer 3   Although inconsistent decision-makers may **appear** to waver between steps 4 and 5, most typically they don't spend enough time and effort on steps 1 and 2.

Answer 4   In an ideal world, all team leaders would be capable of completing all the tasks undertaken by team members. However, modern work can be very complex, and often it just isn't possible to learn to do everything. These days, teams usually include one or more specialists, and the team leader has to find ways of managing such people without necessarily understanding everything they do.

Answer 5   The three responsibilities were to the task, to the individual and to the team.

Answer 6   You might have mentioned:

- supporting and encouraging the individual;
- assigning tasks appropriate to the member's abilities;
- making clear the job roles of the team members;
- assessing performance;
- (if necessary) protecting the individual from other people, including other members of the group.

Answer 7   You could have listed any **three** of the following:

- demonstrating a commitment to the team;
- setting out and agreeing the overall and specific aims and objectives, so that everyone knows what has to be done and why;
- helping to ensure that the standards of the group are maintained;
- supporting the team when things are going against it.

Answer 8   The questions mentioned in the workbook were as follows.

- 'Did you/we reach the task objectives?'
- 'If not, why not: what were the precise reasons for failure? What would you do differently next time? Are the objectives themselves unrealistic?'
- 'If the task was successfully accomplished, what do you think you/we learned? What can we apply to other tasks? Should we set higher targets?'
- 'How well did we work as a team?'
- 'How could we do things better?'

Answer 9   The team think of the team leader first when they think of the organization's management. So far as they are concerned, it is the leader who is empowered to interpret higher management's demands and wishes. In addition, communications from the team would normally go through the leader, as their representative.

Answer 10   The correct matches are as follows.

a Role ambiguity.	y Uncertainty about roles.
b Role underload.	z When an individual feels that he or she is capable of more roles or a bigger role.
c Role incompatibility.	x When different people have different expectations about someone's role.
d Role conflict.	w A clash between what is expected of you in one role and what is expected in another role.

Question 11   The four factors that affect team performance are: the leader, the task, the team and the operational environment.

Question 12   The types of behaviour that overlay the four styles of leadership are authoritative and supportive behaviour. Authoritative behaviour relates to authoritative and consultative leadership styles. Supportive behaviour relates to supportive and delegative leadership styles.

Question 13   The term SMART means that objectives are: Specific, Measurable, Achievable, Relevant and Time bound.

Question 14   Conflict might arise during the storming stage of team development because team members will be exploring boundaries, trying to discover their place on the team and developing their relationships with others and the leader.

Question 15   The skills that are required within the consultative style of leadership are: providing constructive support, facilitating discussion, handling conflict, resolving conflict, listening and reviewing with others.

7 Certificate

Completion of this certificate by an authorized person shows that you have worked through all the parts of this workbook and satisfactorily completed the assessments. The certificate provides a record of what you have done that may be used for exemptions or as evidence of prior learning against other nationally certificated qualifications.

Pergamon Flexible Learning and ILM are always keen to refine and improve their products. One of the key sources of information to help this process are people who have just used the product. If you have any information or views, good or bad, please pass these on.

INSTITUTE OF LEADERSHIP & MANAGEMENT

SUPERSERIES

Leading Your Team

....

has satisfactorily completed this workbook

Name of signatory   ....

Position   ....

Signature   ....

Date   ....

Official stamp

Fourth Edition

INSTITUTE OF LEADERSHIP & MANAGEMENT
SUPER SERIES
FOURTH EDITION

To order – phone us direct for prices and availability details
(please quote ISBNs when ordering) on 01865 888190